WRESTLING SUPERST★RS

# KOFI KINGSTON

BY JESSE ARMSTRONG

BELLWETHER MEDIA • MINNEAPOLIS, MN

**EPIC BOOKS** are no ordinary books. They burst with intense action, high-speed heroics, and shadows of the unknown. Are you ready for an Epic adventure?

This edition first published in 2015 by Bellwether Media, Inc.

No part of this publication may be reproduced in whole or in part without written permission of the publisher. For information regarding permission, write to Bellwether Media, Inc., Attention: Permissions Department, 5357 Penn Avenue South, Minneapolis, MN 55419.

Library of Congress Cataloging-in-Publication Data

Armstrong, Jesse.
  Kofi Kingston / by Jesse Armstrong.
     pages cm. – (Epic. Wrestling Superstars)
Includes bibliographical references and index.
Summary: "Engaging images accompany information about Kofi Kingston. The combination of high-interest subject matter and light text is intended for students in grades 2 through 7"– Provided by publisher.
  Audience: Ages 7-12.
  ISBN 978-1-62617-180-0 (hardcover : alk. paper)
  1. Kingston, Kofi, 1981—Juvenile literature. 2. Wrestlers–United States–Biography–Juvenile literature. 3. Wrestlers–Ghana–Biography–Juvenile literature.  I. Title.
  GV1196.K62A75 2015
  796.812092–dc23
  [B]
                        2014036730

Printed in the United States of America, North Mankato, MN.

# TABLE OF CONTENTS

## WARNING!

The wrestling moves used in this book are performed by professionals.
Do not attempt to reenact any of the moves performed in this book.

# THE DEBUT

Kofi Kingston enters the ring with spirit and a smile. It is his WWE **debut**. The announcers say he is the first Jamaican superstar.

Kingston uses energetic moves on David Owen. He bounces around the ring with ease. He gets the win and excites the fans.

# WHO IS KOFI KINGSTON?

Kofi Kingston is a positive force in WWE. Fans love his flashy moves. Few opponents have his level of **enthusiasm**.

# LIFE BEFORE WWE

Kingston was born in Ghana, West Africa. His family moved to Boston when he was young. He played basketball and wrestled as a kid.

He watched pro wrestling, too.
He practiced moves on his
Bugs Bunny toy.

communications in college. Then he had an **advertising** job for a time. Soon he turned his focus to wrestling.

## FOR THE AUDIENCE

He still uses his college degree. He decides how to present himself and what to wear.

# A WWE SUPERSTAR

## STAR PROFILE

**WRESTLING NAME:** Kofi Kingston

**REAL NAME:** Kofi Nahaje Sarkodie-Mensah

**BIRTHDATE:** August 14, 1981

**HOMETOWN:** Ghana, West Africa

**HEIGHT:** 6 feet (1.8 meters)

**WEIGHT:** 212 pounds (96 kilograms)

**WWE DEBUT:** 2008

**FINISHING MOVE:** Trouble in Paradise

WWE noticed Kingston at the **Chaotic** Training Center in Massachusetts. He pretended to be from Jamaica and had fun moves. In 2006, he signed a **developmental contract**.

In 2008, Kingston won the **Intercontinental** Championship just months after his debut. Since then, he has collected many more individual **titles**. He has also earned **tag team** championships.

EVAN BOURNE

## TEAM NAME

Fans named the team of Kingston and Evan Bourne "Air Boom."

# WINNING MOVES

The Trouble in Paradise has helped with many wins. This **finishing move** is a spin followed by a kick. It takes opponents down.

The Boom Drop is also a strong **signature move**. Kingston jumps up in a sitting position. Then he lands on his opponent. BOOM!

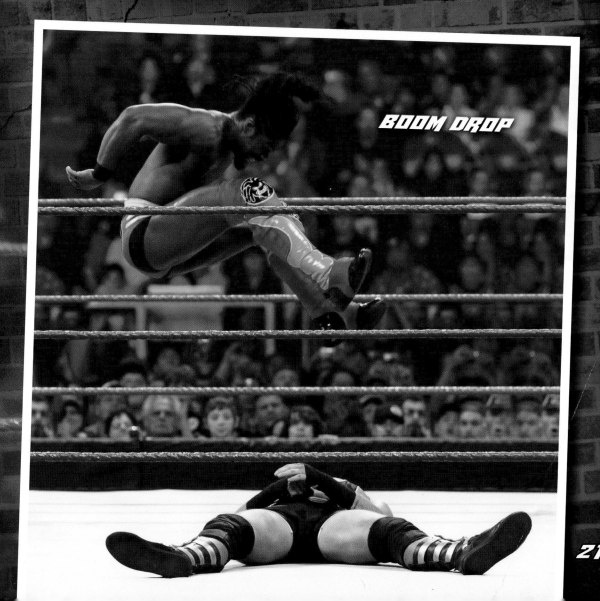

BOOM DROP

# GLOSSARY

**advertising**—the business of presenting products and services to the public

**chaotic**—out of control

**debut**—first official appearance

**developmental contract**—an agreement between WWE and a wrestler; WWE promises to train the wrestler in smaller leagues.

**enthusiasm**—great interest and excitement

**finishing move**—a wrestling move that finishes off an opponent

**intercontinental**—involving more than one continent

**signature move**—a move that a wrestler is famous for performing

**tag team**—a pair of wrestlers who compete as a team

**titles**—championships

# TO LEARN MORE

## At the Library

Armstrong, Jesse. *Randy Orton*. Minneapolis, Minn.: Bellwether Media, 2015.

Black, Jake. *WWE General Manager's Handbook*. New York, N.Y.: Grosset & Dunlap, 2012.

Black, Jake. *WWE Supersized Activity Book*. New York, N.Y.: Grosset & Dunlap, 2012.

## On the Web

Learning more about Kofi Kingston is as easy as 1, 2, 3.

1. Go to www.factsurfer.com.

2. Enter "Kofi Kingston" into the search box.

3. Click the "Surf" button and you will see a list of related web sites.

With factsurfer.com, finding more information is just a click away.

# INDEX

The images in this book are reproduced through the courtesy of: Matt Roberts/ Corbis/ Zuma Press/ Newscom, front cover, pp. 5, 18; Fran Ruchalski, front cover (small), pp. 6, 13; Miguel Discart/ Flickr, p. 4; Wenn Photos/ Newscom, pp. 7, 16; Charley Gallay/ Getty Images, p. 8; Daniel Reyes/ Newscom, p. 10; Paul Cush, p. 11; Erika Goldring/ Getty Images, p. 12; Moses Robinson/ Getty Images, pp. 14, 15; David Seto, pp. 17, 19; Devin Chen, p. 20.